I0159551

A B C'S
OF PEOPLE MANAGEMENT

Dr. Alton E. Loveless

FWB Publications

Columbus, Ohio 43207

FWB

The Process of Leadership

Leadership begins with the desire to achieve

    _to achieve, the leader must set goals
    _to set goals, he must make decisions to achieve
    goals, he must plan
    _to plan, he must analyze
    _to implement, he must organize
    _to organize, he must delegate
    _to delegate, he must administer
    _to administer, he must communicate
    _to communicate, he must motivate
    _to motivate, he must share
    _to share, he must care
    _to care, he must believe
    _to believe, he must set goals that spire belief and
      the desire to achieve

      **Thus, the -"Process of Leadership"
      begins and ends with goals.**

If you want people to go with you,
they must be a part of the decision making process.

People don't do what you expect,
they do what you inspect.

INTRODUCTION

No one has all the answers to leadership. Nor do I. But the following pages are guidelines that helped govern me during my years in attempting to manage people through the various roles of leadership.

The principles that covered my leading were:
- Do nothing merely just because you want to unless it is right and wise, and good.
- Do nothing that you will have to deny you did.
- Do nothing that you will be ashamed of having done.
- Do right.
- Do unto others as you would that they should do to you.
- Be the best scholar you can be.

If the following principles in this will help you in your leadership role, I will accomplish what I desired to do by leaving nearly 60 years of leadership to others.

Table of Contents

1

ALONENESS:
THE ADVERSARY OF LEADERSHIP

Studies conducted by Management Training Systems indicate that 90% of all job turnover is connected with relationship problems. Therefore, maintaining good relationships is important to organizational stability and productivity.

WHAT YOU SHOULD KNOW ABOUT RELATIONSHIPS
- All relationships revolve around personal needs.
- Contact alters relationships.
- Relationships are constantly changing.
- Met needs build relationships.
- Unmet needs erode relationships.

THE FOUR RELATIONSHIP STYLES
There are four basic relationship styles: Cooperation. Retaliation. Domination and Isolation. All relationships begin in a Cooperation style and remain there as long as all needs within the relationship are being met.

An unmet need causes the person with the need to move to a Retaliation style of relationship in an effort to get his or her need met. This relationship style focuses on a struggle to get the other person to meet the unmet need.

Eventually, there is what appears to be a winner and a loser. At this point, a new relationship begins called Domination. During this period of the relationship, the person losing the struggle for control is dominated by the person "winning" the struggle.

After a period of time, the person being dominated concludes he is being rejected and the situation is hopeless. At this point, he takes the first step to a new relationship style--Isolation. An Isolation relationship style is the last phase of a deteriorating relationship before termination.

Leaders and members are in one of these four relationship styles with people at all times. The farther one moves away from a Cooperation style the lower productivity drops.

The greatest level of satisfaction is maintained within the Cooperation style. Therefore, the leader must focus on maintaining an atmosphere of cooperation within his team or workgroup and membership.

Let us take a look at the conditions that vary in the four relationship styles that follow. And in addition needless to say that even we find ourselves in any of the following.

Conditions within the COOPERATION STYLE

- There will be a commitment to meet the other person's needs.
- Mutual trust and respect will exist.
- There will be a mutual utilization of personal skills and creativity.
- Problems will be solved jointly.
- Productivity will increase.
- Commitment to the relationship will grow.

Conditions within the RETALIATION STYLE

The Retaliation style contains the following conditions:

- There are attempts to make the other person conform to what you want to be done.
- Aggressive action toward the other person is eventually taken.
- The other person becomes an object in your way and not a person with his own needs.
- A struggle for domination begins.
- There is a period of perpetual conflict.
- Eventually, there appears to be a winner and loser.

Conditions within the DOMINATION STYLE

The Domination style contains the following conditions:

- The "losers controlled by the "winner."
- The loser's personality is "suffocated."
- Each loses respect for the other.
- The loser's creativity is lost.
- The loser resorts to manipulation.
- The loser gives up--concludes the situation is hopeless--and the relationship will not improve.

Conditions within ISOLATION STYLE

The following conditions exist within the Isolation style:

- The other person is mentally blocked out.
- Communication stops.
- Both develop a mistrust of the other.
- Problems remain unsolved.
- Needs remain unmet.
- Each develops unconcern for the other's needs.
- Productivity within the relationship drops drastically.
- Relationship terminates.

RESTORING RELATIONSHIPS
back to cooperation

The key to maintaining good relationships is to know what to do when the relationship starts to deteriorate.

No one is immune from relationship problems. The mature person faces them when they occur and commits himself to finding a solution.

RULES FOR RIGHT RELATIONSHIPS

In order to maintain a Cooperation style relationship apply the following rules:

Attack the problem...not the person. If you attack the person instead of the problem you will cause the relationship to move out of cooperation into retaliation.

Verbalize feelings...don't act them out. State how you feel and why, instead of communicating your feelings by the way you act.

Forgive in place of judging. When you are wronged forgive the person involved. Don't judge the person for his actions.

Be committed to *giving more than you take*. The key to a cooperation relationship is giving more than you take. Always focus on meeting the needs of the other person. If everyone in the relationship does this all needs will continually be met.

Loneliness is perhaps the strongest foe many of us will ever face. It creates the sensation of being cut off, of being isolated from those who are closest and most important to you, and of having no meaningful relationship with anyone who truly cares. People often feel lonely even with family and friends nearby.

There is a difference between loneliness and aloneness. Being alone can be depressing, but it can also be used to minister to your spirit and feelings in an intimate way. Aloneness can be good and beneficial, while loneliness is hard for any of us to take.

Only you can control the extent of your loneliness. You can choose to remain melancholy and depressed, or you can focus on brighter things.

2

BEHAVIOR:
THE BASIS OF PROPER RELATIONSHIPS

Human Behavior Is Manageable

One of the most important things to learn about managing people is all people can be led but all are different. Therefore let me present some concepts that I learned during my years of managing people.

Let us first look at the role in which you perform your task and how people perceive who you are and how they will follow. They may see you in an entirely different way than you see yourself. Take a moment and READ the outline I have set forth.

1. Requirements for those who lead
 A). Authority by which a leader manages
  1). The authority of competence
  2). The authority of position
  3). The authority of your personality
  4). The authority of character

B). Steps in effective leading and direction
    1). Communication
    2). Faith and confidence in one's own ability
    3). Faith and confidence in other people
    4). Knowledge of human nature and behavior
    5). Proper delegation
    6). Trestle and bridge-building.
      (Public relations)

C). What a leader must prepare in advance
    1). Establish a system for evaluating personnel, workers or followers
    2). Establish a system of checks and controls
    3). Establish a system of motivation and rewards
    4). Establish a system of discipline
    5). Ensure that the ideas, people, things, time, and other elements of leadership will be available at the right time, in the right place, in the right quantities

2. Relationship with those who are led
    1) Appreciate people for who they are
    2) Anticipate they will do their best
    3) Admire their accomplishments
    4) Accept your personal responsibility

I continue to be amazed at how some football coaches are able to take some of the most diversified players and make them winners. The following I recall from the coach of Alabama years ago.

I'm just a plow hand from Arkansas, but I have learned how to hold a team together--how to lift some men up, how to calm down others until finally, they've got one heartbeat together, a team. There are just three things I'd ever say: If anything goes bad, I did it. If anything goes semi-good, then we did it. If anything goes really good, then you did it. That's all it takes to get people to win football games for you. --Bear Bryant

There are six basic types of problems that I have discovered in leading people.
    1). Problems with ideas
    2). Problems with people
    3). Problems with things
    4). Problems with time
    5). Problems with leadership
    6). Problems with faith
You may discover more as you develop your leadership.

Effective and good leaders will learn early on that Leadership may be used in three ways:
    1). Doing things "to" the people
    2). Doing things "for" the people
    3). Doing things "through" the people

Resistance from those who labor
If you could change one thing. What would it be? Would it be a change in facilities, scheduling, curriculum, organization, personnel, equipment, or training? If you made all these changes at once what would be the results or reactions?

LET ME LIST FOR YOU WHY PEOPLE RESIST CHANGE.

1). *Loss of security*.
- The unknown, the unfamiliar are frightening and unpredictable.
- The new and different are strange and uncomfortable.
- The familiar is preferred.
- People like to know what to expect.
- Change may result in loss of security.

2). *Threatened personal status or position.*
- An Individual's vested interest may appear to be at stake.
- Even something as simple as changing from one place to another may cause resistance.

3). *Implied criticism of the present.*
- New ideas suggest dissatisfaction with the way things are done now.
- It may suggest that the old way is not good enough (which it may not be).
- Yet many people are satisfied with the status quo.

4). *Seems unnecessary* or *unhelpful*.
- For some the present situation is satisfactory.
- For others, it's utterly hopeless.
- Or an idea may be resisted because something similar was tried before without success.

> Two words that can kill any new ideas are <u>never</u> and <u>always</u>, as in "We never did it that way before," or "'We always did it this way."

Let me share with you what I did in attempting to prevent resistance to change. And you may struggle during this same time since it will determine how effective you are. Credibility always takes time even though the sign on your door is Boss.

In spite of your best efforts, resistance to change will probably exist. How can you handle it? There are seven possibilities.

First, you can feel that the opposition is a personal threat and resign from your position with hurt feelings.

Second, you can forcibly impose the change. In spite of resistance and lose your co-workers' confidence and cooperation. If you follow this approach, begin looking for a new staff of workers.

Third, remember all resistance is not bad. It may force you to reevaluate the proposed change. You may change it, strengthen, and improve it.

Fourth, express understanding from an opposite viewpoint. Try to see the situation from the other person's vantage point.

Fifth, Admit strength in *others' positions.* Realize that no idea is all good or all bad. If you admit the good points, the opposition may admit yours.

Sixth, *Evaluate objections with the individual.* Think through each argument point-for-point. It may reveal the weaknesses of the objection.

Seventh, *when the opposition is intense. Shift into neutral.* Don't try to win every issue. You may win a point and lose the respect and services of an otherwise good worker. Anything worthwhile is worth waiting for.

Let me suggest ideas when you are presenting new ideas and changes.

What can you do to help people feel the need for change and accept it more readily?

1).Carefully present there exists a sense of dissatisfaction with the status quo. Periodically evaluate programs and structures. Let the facts speak for themselves. Use your records to point out a need for change. Chart attendance for the year. Compare it with the previous year. Let the facts speak.

2). *Let people share in planning for change.* People will more likely accept change if they think a new idea is theirs or that they were involved in the planning.

I learned many years ago that if you want people to go with you they have to be a part of the decision-making process.

3). *Give forewarning of any proposed change.* Don't spring new ideas and changes on people. Keep them informed as the change takes place.

4). *Begin by making* small *changes.* Sweeping revisions can start with a simple step in the right direction

There are some rules for you to learn when you are presenting a new idea. Below are five things that governed me:

1). *Don't oversell* it. **Avoid high-pressure tactics**.

2). *Watch your timing.* Be aware of extenuating circumstances that might affect the outcome. Take note of' the group atmosphere and attitudes.

3). *Be positive.* **Stress the advantages.** List the pros and cons and try to answer objections in your presentation.

4). *Give people* a *chance* to *think it over* and talk about it. Give them a chance to get used to the new idea.

5). *Pray* for *each new idea.* Rely on the Holy Spirit to break down barriers. Open closed minds. Dissolve resistance and create a readiness to change.

As a leader who encourages people to accept and adjust to change be *personable.* Be human. Exhibit a spirit of humility. Win and hold their respect. Express personal interest in others as individuals. Keep a sense of humor. Don't take yourself too seriously.

You can change things and live to talk about it!

Let me share with you something given to me that would help you in your relationship with others.

THE TEN COMMANDMENTS OF HUMAN RELATIONS.

1. SPEAK TO PEOPLE. There is nothing as nice as a cheerful word of greeting.

2. SMILE AT PEOPLE. It takes 72 muscles to frown and only 14 to smile.

3. CALL PEOPLE BY NAME. The sweetest music to many ears is the sound of one's own name.

4. BE FRIENDLY AND HELPFUL. If you would have friends, be friendly.

5. BE CORDIAL. Speak and act as though everything you do is a genuine pleasure.

6. HAVE A GENUINE INTEREST IN PEOPLE.

7. BE GENEROUS WITH PRAISE. CAUTIOUS WITH CRITICISM.

8. BE CONSIDERATE OF THE FEELINGS OF OTHERS. There are three sides to a controversy: yours, the other side, and the right one.

9. BE THOUGHTFUL OF THE OPINIONS OF OTHERS.

10. BE ALERT TO GIVE SERVICE. What counts most in life is what we do for others.

HUMAN BEHAVIOR CAN BE MOTIVATED

Understanding motivation

A). Motivation is psychological, not logical

B). Motivation is fundamentally an unconscious process

C). Motivation is an individual matter

D). Motivating needs differ from person to person

E). Motivation is inevitably a social process

Motivation is person related. Take some time and absorb each of the following to learn about taking people from one point to another.

- Behavior depends on both the person and his environment.
- Each individual behaves in ways which make sense to him.
- An individual's perception of a situation influences his behavior in that situation.
- An individual's view of himself influences what he does.
- An individual's behavior is influenced by his needs.
- Everyone is motivated at some level.
- Motivation always involves some goal.
- Motivations are learned not inherited.
- Human desires precede motivation.
- Motivation is more effective when a man has a clear concept of his goal.

- Motivation is inseparable from one's values, needs, and desires.
- Motivation begins where the person is.
- Information regarding a goals distance is motivation.
- The "terms" of one's motivation are "defined" by the individual.
- One's self-image is related to the direction and limits of his motivation.

Learn How to motivate

- Communicate standards (be consistent)
- Be aware Of your own biases and prejudices
- Let people know where they stand
- Give praise when it is appropriate
- Keep people informed of changes that may affect them
- Care about your people
- Perceive people as ends, not means
- Go out of your way to help people
- Take responsibility for your people
- Build independence
- Exhibit personal diligence

Please note some things that keep you from motivating people or may destroy your effectiveness as a leader.

- Never belittle a subordinate
  (Destroys self-worth)
- Never criticize a subordinate in front of others
  (Destroys rapport)
- Give subordinate your undivided attention
  (Self-respect disappears)
- Never seem preoccupied with your own interests
  (Gives impression of selfishness and manipulation of others for your own purposes)
- Never play favorites
  (Destroys morale)
- Never fail to help your sub-ordinates grow
- Never be insensitive to small things
- Never embarrass weak followers
- Never vacillate in making a Decision

The following are some of the things that motivate people.

- As they see their own Achievement.
- When there is Recognition for their accomplishments.
- When they enjoy the Work itself.
- When they are given Responsibility.
- When he earns an Advancement.
- The Working conditions and environment.

Human behavior is often misunderstood

Realities about a misunderstanding. Trying to understand people is one of the most difficult things one will find as he leads others. I will share some that I encountered along my way.

- Misunderstanding is rarely the fault of any one person
- Misunderstanding is seldom voluntary
- Misunderstanding is always preceded by some cause
- Misunderstanding usually affects, both parties
- Misunderstanding regardless of severity need not mean the termination of what was previously a wholesome relationship

Here are some reasons for misunderstanding:

- Our experiences are different
- Our perceptions of ourselves are different
- Our images of others are different
- Our needs and wants are different
- Our values are different
- Our problems are different
- Our secrets are different
- Our definitions are different
- Our abilities to communicate are different
- Our perceptions of expectations from others are different
- What we see is different
- We think others are like us
- Misinterpretations of intermediaries cause misunderstanding

3

COMMUNICATION:
THE CRAFT OF CREATING UNITY

What is communication? Most people admit they have communication problems from time to time. But few people clearly understand what communication is. Communication can be defined as *the process we go through* to *convey understanding from one* person or *group* to *another.* Unless understanding occurs we have not communicated.

Understanding the Communication Process

Step One: *Develop* a clear Concept *of the* Idea a- *feeling* to be *communicated.* All communication focuses on the transmitting of Ideas and/or feelings. If a person doesn't know what he is trying to say. The people receiving the message will not understand what he is saying.

Step Two: *Choose the right* words *and actions* to *convey the* Idea *and/or feeling.* Ideas and feelings are transmitted through words and actions. Therefore. It Is Important to make sure right words and actions are used in transmitting the desired message. The wrong action or word can distort the message. Causing misunderstanding.

Step Three: *(The* barriers to *communication).* A series of barriers stand in the way of sending a message and receiving what was said. These barriers may vary slightly from organization to organization and person to person. It Is Important to Identify and eliminate them In order to develop and maintain effective communication.

Step Four: The *listener receives the information.* The Listener or receiver of the Information plays a very important role in the development of understanding. His first Job is to listen to the Ideas and feelings being transmitted to him. Therefore. Listening plays a very important role In the process of developing understanding. More will be said about this later.

Step Five: The *receiver translates words* and *actions into ideas* and *feelings:* The translation of words and actions Into Ideas and feelings is a very critical step in the development of understanding. A great deal of the Idea and feeling can be lost during this phase of the process.

Step Six: The *receiver develops* an *idea* and *feeding.* If the idea and feeling being sent In step one Is the same idea and feeling being received in step six. Understanding occurs and those involved have communicated effectively. On the other hand. if the idea and feeling in step six are different than the idea and feeling sent In step one, we have the misunderstanding and no communication. Therefore, the goal is to make sure the idea and feeling sent is the idea and Feeling received. This is accomplished by feeding back the ideas and Feelings heard.

A. The importance of disclosure and feedback

Honesty in the form of being willing to disclose true ideas and feelings plays an important part in the development of understanding between individuals and groups. The person unwilling to disclose his ideas and feelings cannot experience effective communication. Honest disclosure makes known to others what is known to you. On the other hand. Feedback from others allows you to know what others know. Without disclosure and feedback, people cannot experience good communication.

B. The role of non-verbal communication

Studies have shown that most ideas and feelings are transmitted non-verbally. This means what you "do" communicates far more than what you "say".

Most Messages are communicated in the following way:
55% of the message Is communicated non-verbally.
38% Is communicated through tone of voice.
7% is communicated by actual words.

This means that 93% of all Ideas and feelings are communicated through some form of non-verbal means-- either actions or the way we say a word. Therefore. How you say a word becomes more important than the word itself. This also indicates that most of the misunderstanding is communication occurs within the non-verbal area of communication.

C. The importance of perceptive listening

Since 93% of the message Is communicated non-verbally. It becomes extremely important for the listener to make sure he translates the message properly. For example. in Mark 8:11-21 It Is obvious the disciples had misunderstood Jesus. Part of It was due to improper listening. Therefore. Listening skills play a very important role in the development of understanding.

D. Passive listening vs. Perceptive listening

The person using "passive" listening Is only hearing the words being spoken. Therefore. he receives approximately 7% of the true Ideas and feelings being transmitted. Passive listening always fails to hear the meaning. Ideas and feelings behind the words being spoken.

On the other hand. Perceptive listening focuses on the actions and tone of voice as well as the meaning. Attitudes and feelings behind the words being spoken. The person using perceptive listening hears far more than just the words being spoken. He also hears the other 93% of the message that is being transmitted non-verbally. It has been said. "Words do not have to mean. People have to mean for words." That is why every person needs to learn to use a perceptive Listening skill. Perceptive Listening allows the person to hear the real meaning attached to the words being used to communicate Ideas and feelings.

E. Attitudes needed when using perceptive listening

The person using perceptive listening techniques must want to hear the real feelings and attitudes of the person sending the message. He must also be willing to accept the attitudes and feelings being communicated. And finally, he must have a desire to assist in any way possible.

The person unwilling to accept the real feelings of others and help where needed is wasting his or her time using perceptive listening skills.

The ten worst listening habits given below are but signs of everyone's lack of proper communication.

This was from a poll of freshmen and sophomores at the Universities of Wisconsin and Minnesota.

The first bad listening habit given was to **"Declare The Subject Uninteresting."** A lot of us store up mental tangents of "How dull can this be?" Just to use in moments of boredom. However, one can introduce the one little thought of "How much can I use from this subject?" Needless to say, the good listener is a sifter, a screener, a winnower of the wheat from the chaff, always hunting something worthwhile or practical which he can store and use in the days ahead.

G. K. Chesterton put it beautifully when he said, *"In all the world there is no such thing as an uninteresting subject. There are only uninterested subjects."*

The second bad listening habit was **"Criticizing The Speaker's Delivery."** The bad listener always finds something to belittle a speaker in his mind. "Is this the best they can do?" "This man can't even talk." "All he does is read his notes." "He doesn't even look at his audience." "What a terrible voice!"

A good listener moves with the attitude, "This person knows something I don't know or he wouldn't be up there." Remember, learning and listening are an inside action on the part of the listener. The speaker is doing very little of the learning. The message is 10 times more important as the clothing in which it comes.

Thirdly, a poor listening habit is, **"Getting Overstimulated."** Some people get so excited about some people or things they can't control themselves. This is triggered when a speaker begins to develop his topic and suddenly the listener feels he has walked rough-shod on one of his pet biases or convictions. Then, he will sit there and gnash his teeth figuring out the best possible way to embarrass the speaker.

All too often has that person sat for 30 minutes then found an opportunity to query the speaker only to have him return in complete wonderment with, "Didn't you hear my answer to that question minutes ago?"

A good listener withholds evaluation until comprehension is complete. In other words, it says, "Hear the man out before you judge him."

Bad listening habit number four was **"Listening Only For Facts."** Researchers say listeners listen with only about 25% efficiency. Thusly, most people who listen only for facts; get a few, garbled a shocking number, but completely lost most. The good listener tries to get the gist of each main idea. It can be noted that facts can be retained only when they make sense, and they make sense only when they support a generalization of some kind.

The fifth poor listening habit is **"Outlining Everything."** Many people think note-taking and outlining are synonyms. There is nothing wrong with outlining if the speaker is following an outline pattern of organization. Unfortunately, most speakers don't outline and before we realize that fact, most of a lesson is gone and we find ourselves in a frustration while we tried to determine his discourse points.

One good way to take notes is to draw a line down the middle of a paper and write facts on one side and principles on the other, both at the top. Listen to the speaker for a few minutes noting facts then write a one-sentence summary of what he is trying to get you to understand. Keep an attitude of the speaker, "I'm ready, produce! Speaker, produce!"

Sixth, **"Faking Attention"** ranks high in most of our poor listening habits.

Having paid the speaker, the overt courtesy of appearing to tune him in, the listener feels conscience free to take off into a thousand mental directions. Efficient listening is characterized by a quicker action of the heart, a faster circulation of blood, a small rise in body temperature. The attention forced becomes a collection of tensions inside the listener who has resolved to get the facts and ideas the speaker is trying to convey.

Seventh is **"Tolerating Or Creating Distractions".**

Eighth is **"Evading The Difficult".** Most poor listeners had rather avoid any different situation of presentations according to research. This contributes to their "inexperienced status". The wise listener sees everything hard as a challenge and soon learns it is just often as easy as the simple.

Ninth, **"Submitting To Emotion Laden Words."** It is not known what words affect everyone, but it is known that some are effective in affecting many. It is silly how sometimes a simple word—merely a symbol of something can get us so excited as to disrupt our listening efficiently. (Do you know what words affect your emotions?)

Tenth, the **"Wasting Of Thought Power".** I have left it until last because I think it could far be the most important. An average teacher talks about 125 words per minute but a listener has an easy cruising speed of at least 400-500 words a minute. The difference between speech speed and thought speed can operate as a tremendous pitfall.

Thought power does not have to be wasted. If you can think four times faster than a man can talk, you surely have a source power; it should not be a weakness.

The process of converting the speakers' words becomes the business of learning. What things do you engage in mentally in order to stay tuned in on the speech?

May I suggest three:

(1) Anticipate the speaker's next comment. Dash ahead of him and to guess what his next main point is likely to be. If you guess it, learning is reinforced. If you guess wrong, you can compare his reasoning with yours. That is one of the oldest laws of learning-that of comparison and contrast.

(2) Identify elements. The average speaker uses only three ways to build points. He explains the point, or gets emotional and harangue the point or he illustrates the point with a factual generalization following the illustration. A good listener knows this and spends the differential between the thought speed and speech speed to identify what is being used as a point support material.

(3) Make mental summaries. Throw in periodic mental summaries.

4

POWER PACKED WORDS

Many psychologists agree that certain words have an emotional or rational impact on people.

Do you remember to an old saying, "Words don't have meanings, we give meaning to words?"

The Importance of Language

As a leader, speaker, or writer, it is important not only to think about *what* you say but *how* you say it.

To communicate effectively, it is not enough to have well-organized ideas expressed in complete and coherent sentences and paragraphs. One must also think about the style, tone, and clarity of his use of words, and adapt these elements to those he is addressing. Again, analyzing one's usage and purpose is the key to effectiveness.

In order to choose the most effective language, a person must consider the objective, the context in which it is being given, and who will be using it.

Characteristics of Effective Language

There are six main characteristics of effective language.
Effective language is:
(1) Concrete and Specific, Not Vague and Abstract
(2) Concise, Not Verbose
(3) Familiar, Not Obscure
(4) Precise and Clear, Not Inaccurate or Ambiguous
(5) Constructive, Not Destructive
(6) Appropriately Formal.

Some words almost automatically have a strong appeal, no matter how they're used. Communications experts have tried to identify these power-laden words and their research has proven valuable to salesmen, advertising men, politicians, and anyone trying to influence other people. One of the earliest and most complete lists of emotion-packed words was drawn up by a noted psychologist, many of whose suggestions are included in the following new list:

How many of these words can you include in your usage?

1.	Scientific	31.	Hunting
2.	Durable	32.	Status
3.	Clean	*33.	New
4.	Efficient	34.	Enormous
5.	Time-saving	35.	Low-cost
*6.	Proven	36.	Genuine
7.	Value	37.	Progress
8.	Fun	38.	Thinking
9.	Ambition	39.	Excel
*10.	Love	40.	Integrity

11.	Reputation	41.	Engineered
*12.	Guaranteed	42.	Recommended
13.	Stimulating	43.	Rugged
14.	Safe	*44.	You
15.	Popular	45.	Stylish
16.	Economical	46.	Admired
17.	Mother	47.	Innovation
18.	Modern	*48.	Money
*19.	Health	49.	Beauty
20.	Quality	50.	Personality
21.	Elegance	51.	Independent
22.	Bargain	52.	Successful
23.	Sympathy	53.	Up-to-date
*24.	Easy	54.	Tested
25.	Necessary	*55.	Save
26.	Home	56.	Relief
27.	Courtesy	57.	Tasteful
28.	Growth	*58.	Results
29.	Versatile	*59.	Free
30.	Obligation	*60.	Discovery

Did you notice any numbers with a *? They are considered by those who are rhetoric experts and marketers as the 12 most powerful words in the English language.

You should learn to use these and the positive words below in your leadership and management and avoid the negative words listed later.

POSITIVE WORDS

Most people like these words:

ability	joy	service
achieve	judgment	smile
advantage	kind	success
agree	knack	think
beauty	lasting	thrive
benefit	lovely	truth
character	maximum	understand
charming	music	unity
comprehensive	news	useful
determined	opportunity	valuable
economy	pleasant	victory
fun	productive	vigorous
good	profit	warm
guarantee	pure	wholesome
health	reasonable	winning
helpful	rejoice	wonderful
holiday	reliable	you
ideal	satisfy	youthful
industrious	save	

NEGATIVE WORDS

People usually dislike words:

absurd	crooked	laborious
ridicule	deadlock	guilty
allege	unwieldy	liar
standstill	destroy	loathsome
avenge	discredit	lowborn
awkward	disorder	suspicious
backward	disrepute	prejudiced
barb	tragic	hardship
bewilder	ugly	hate
blame	delay	hoodwink
blunder	vaunt	hopeless
bury	waste	humiliate
careless	wrong	hurt
meaningless	drudgery	illicit
mistake	dupe	imperfect
nefarious	embezzle	inconvenience
obnoxious	embitter	insanely
obstacle	encroach	insolvent
offend	enmity	killing
pain	enrage	poor
complain	error	liable
condemn	exaggerate	alibi
contrary	failure	ruin
counterfeit	fearful	attack
coward	flaunt	maim
crazy	gloomy	threat

5

Developing
C H A R I S M A

Charisma

C-oncern -the ability to show you care

H-elp -the ability to reach out

A- ction -the ability to make things happen

R-esults -the ability to produce influence -the ability to lead sensitivity -the Ability to feel/respond

M-otivation -the ability to give hope affirmation -the ability to build up.

> Be more concerned about making others feel good about themselves than you are in making them feel good about you.

A-sk yourself what draws you to people? Try to understand and develop the qualities you enjoy in others

Five ways you want <u>others </u>to treat you
- You want others to encourage
- You want others to appreciate
- You want others to forgive you
- You want others to listen to you
- Want others to understand you

Do you know what draws people to you?
Evaluate what people like about you and why.

6

DEALING WITH CRITICISM

Before you attempt to give criticism to another take a look at the following:

- Check your motive
- Make sure the issue is worthy of criticism
- Be specific
- Don't undermine the person's self- confidence
- Don't compare one person with another
- Be creative or attack the problem not the person and wait until the time is right
- Look at yourself before looking at others

You should always end a meeting with encouragement.
A little self-examination doesn't hurt. I have learned that:

- Leaders have a problem with not being able to take criticism.
- No one has the right to give it if they are unable to receive it in return.
- Each of us learns from others and it can be a valuable teaching experience.
- Become a person who can handle criticism
- Learn to use to use this type of confrontation as an opportunity to grow

How to take criticism

- Understand the difference between constructive and destructive criticism
- Don't take yourself too seriously
- Look beyond the criticism and see the critic
- Watch your attitude toward the critic
- Realize that good people get criticized
- Don't just see the critic: see if there's a crowd
- Wait for time to prove them wrong
- Concentrate on your mission--change your mistakes.

A wise man advised me once about how to take criticism with the following:

- **Listen** to it
- **Learn** from it
- **Love** through it
- **Live** above it

Supervision or management is done with *"no partiality"*. The word "partiality" refers to favoritism. Those in charge are not to show a preference for the position, rank, popularity, or earthly circumstances of any man or woman.

Please YOURSELF by treating your followers fairly and compassionately.

www.ingramcontent.com/pod-product-compliance
Lightning Source LLC
Chambersburg PA
CBHW060629030426
42337CB00018B/3269